Sarah.

JUNIOR SURVIVAL LIBRARY

Close Relatives
THE MONKEY
AND
THE APE

Malcolm Penny

ANGLIA
Television Limited

B⊞XTREE

Key to abbreviations

lb	pound
gm	gramme
kg	kilogram
in	inch
ft	foot
yd	yard
cm	centimetre
m	metre
km	kilometre
sq mile	square mile
sq km	square kilometre
HBL	head and body length
TL	tail length

First published in 1991 by Boxtree Limited
Copyright © 1991 Survival Anglia Limited
Text copyright © 1991 Malcolm Penny

Front jacket photograph:
Survival Anglia/Nick Gordon
(Chimpanzee in a rain-forest in Sierra Leone,
West Africa)
Back jacket photograph:
Survival Anglia/Joanna Van Gruisen
(Capped langurs)

Line drawings by Wayne Ford

A CIP catalogue entry
for this book is available
from the British Library

ISBN 1-85283-331-9

Edited by Cheryl Brown
Designed by Glynn M. Pickerill
Typeset by Rowland Phototypesetting Limited
Bury St Edmunds, Suffolk

Printed and bound in Italy
by OFSA s.p.a.

for Boxtree Limited,
36 Tavistock Street,
London WC2E 7PB

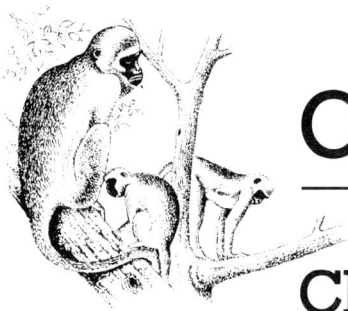

Contents

Climbing the family tree

Biologists divide the animal kingdom into large groups called orders. For example, all the rodents, such as rats, mice, rabbits and so on, are in one order, and all the whales are in another. The last order in the animal kingdom is called the primates, which means 'top animals'. The order of primates contains three groups of closely-related animals: monkeys, apes and humans.

The lesser bushbaby, found all over Africa, is a prosimian. [HBL 16 cm (6½ in); TL 23 cm (9 in)].

The first person to realize that humans had **evolved** from monkeys and apes was a biologist called Charles Darwin. When he published his famous book *The Origin of Species* in 1859 an enormous argument broke out. Many people were sure that humans and other animals could not be related at all: they especially disliked the idea that their ancestors were apes. However the idea is now accepted by most people, though there are still some who disagree in spite of the evidence.

There are 182 different **species** of animal in the primate order ranging from the tiny bushbaby, through the monkeys, to, at the top of the family tree, apes and humans. Although there are many differences between the types of animals in this group, all primates have certain features in common. They have good eyesight, and a large brain for their size. They are able to grasp things with their hands, an adaptation which began with climbing trees, but which eventually enabled some of them to use tools and even, in the case of humans, to write. Primates take a long time to become **adult**. While they are growing up, they are able to learn complicated **social** behaviour, which gives them an advantage over most other animals that are not so good at working together.

The simplest primates, at the bottom of the family tree, are the **prosimians**, a name which means 'almost monkey'. There are 35 species of prosimians including all the lemurs and lorises. They usually move about on all fours.

A golden-headed lion tamarin, a New World monkey from Brazil. Only a very few survive.

They have long snouts, with a good sense of smell, and they have a smaller brain than monkeys and apes. In fact they look more like dogs than monkeys. Those that run about on the large branches of trees even have claws rather like dogs. Other prosimians have nails instead, with long fingers for gripping small branches as they move through the trees.

Next come the monkeys, which can be divided into two groups: the **Old World** monkeys and the **New World** monkeys. The Old World monkeys are found in Africa and Asia, while the New World monkeys are found in Central and South America. Apart from their distribution, the most important difference between these two groups is that

The Barbary macaque is an Old World monkey found in Gibraltar and North Africa.

New World monkeys have a **prehensile** tail: that is a tail which can be used as a fifth limb for grasping.

At the top of the family tree are the most advanced primates—the apes and human beings. Generally speaking an ape is a tailless monkey; but this group can be further divided into gibbons and the great apes—that is the gorilla, the orang-utan and the chimpanzee.

Monkeys and apes often move about in an upright position. They have flexible fingers with pads at the tips to improve their grip: they also have a thumb placed so that it can touch the tips of all the other fingers. This opposable thumb enables them to handle things very delicately when they want to. They have flattened faces, with short snouts,

and the eyes placed in the front, so that they have **binocular** vision: their eyesight is more important to them than their sense of smell.

The ability to stand upright was useful at first for climbing and swinging among trees, but it had another very important effect on the higher primates as they evolved. Animals which go on all fours need powerful muscles to hold their heads up, and thick bones in their skull where the muscles join on. Therefore, by standing upright, monkeys and apes could have thinner skulls, leaving more room for the brain, and so they were able to evolve into

New World monkeys, like these black-handed spider monkeys, can use their tails to pick up small objects.

The long arms of the siamang, a type of gibbon from Indonesia, help it to swing through the trees.

Below *An opposable thumb enables a primate to carry out delicate movements with its hand.*

highly intelligent animals. It also meant that they could develop proper hands, because they no longer needed front feet.

Eventually the large brains and great intelligence of the higher primates led to the evolution of a species of primate which could use language to write down complicated ideas; and others of the species could read and learn about them. This particular species is the only one which has any knowledge of its past history. It evolved to be so different from its ancestors that, as we have seen, some of its members refused to believe that they were descended from monkeys and apes. Yet human beings would not be where they are today if they had not passed through all the stages which brought primates to the top of the evolutionary tree.

A land apart

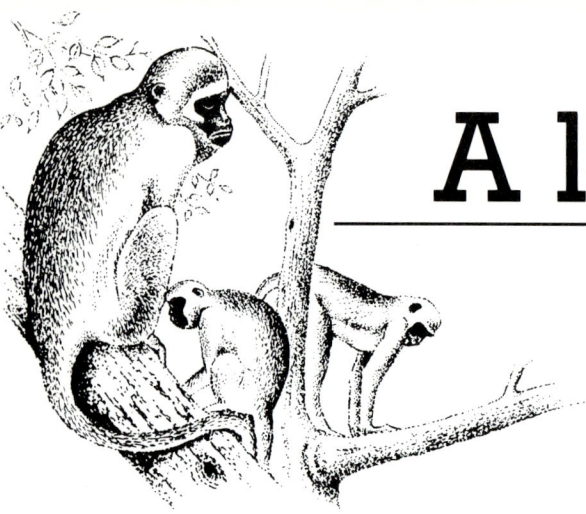

The large island of Madagascar was cut off from the east coast of Africa by a deep channel 100 million years ago. Since then, the animals and plants on the island have evolved along a different route from those in the rest of Africa. Among the animals cut off by the sea were some primitive primates called lemurs.

Although they are prosimians, or 'lower' primates, some groups of lemurs are more like higher primates. There are small, tree-living animals such as the mouse lemur and the lepilemur, which live rather like monkeys (though they look more like tiny dogs!); and then there are others such as the indri and the sifaka which are more like apes such as gibbons and chimpanzees. After all those millions of years, the lemurs evolved into at least 35 different species, all of them found only on Madagascar, and many of them now **extinct**.

A sifaka is a large, agile lemur which lives in deciduous forests.

Left *The small lepilemur feeds by night on leaves, fruit and barks.*

People first came to Madagascar about 2,000 years ago. They began to cut down the forests where the lemurs lived to clear fields to grow crops. Not only did the Malagasy people destroy large areas of the lemurs' natural **habitat**, but they also hunted them for food. Scientists have found the bones of about 15 species of extinct lemur, and many of the surviving species are in great danger.

The smaller species, like the black lemurs and the brown lemurs, live like monkeys in family groups in the forest, where they feed on fruit and leaves. The ring-tailed lemur lives in tribes; individuals in the group keep in contact in the dark forest by waving their

Ring-tailed lemurs use their tails to keep warm as well as for signalling to each other. [HBL 39–48 cm (16–19 in); TL 50–60 cm (20–24 in).]

striped tails at each other. One of the larger species of lemur, the sifaka, lives among the sharp thorns of the spiny forest, a type of vegetation found only on Madagascar. Sifakas, like indris, can often be heard howling, probably to warn other members of the group or to lay claim to territory.

The aye-aye is one the strangest-looking lemurs. It has a thick woolly coat, but large, naked bat-like ears. It has huge incisors and a very long, thin middle finger on each hand, which it uses to prise grubs from under the bark of trees, rather as a woodpecker uses its bill.

The aye-aye is now very rare, because many Malagasy people are afraid of it and kill it on sight. Other species of lemur such as the indri are protected by the Malagasy people, because they regard them as the spirits of their ancestors. They refer to them as: 'Our fathers in the forest'.

The true monkeys

The 'true' or 'typical' monkeys is the name sometimes given to a group of monkey species which includes the macaques and the guenons (often called simply 'monkeys'), the mangabeys and the baboons. The true monkeys are all Old World monkeys: that is they can all be found in Africa and Asia.

Japanese macaques, or snow monkeys, keep warm in winter by bathing in hot springs.

A common characteristic of the true monkeys is their intelligence: they can adapt their behaviour to suit a new way of life in order to survive. The Japanese macaque is a good example of this. Although it is a forest animal by nature, the pressure of the expanding human population in part of its **range** forced some animals to move into the mountains. During the short summer they managed quite well, but when winter came they had to

change their diet, learning to eat tree bark and to dig up roots instead of eating familiar fruits. They also found a remarkable way of keeping warm. They moved into a place in the mountains where there are hot springs, and they made a habit of taking a long hot bath every day during the winter.

The same species of macaque has also shown great skill in learning new behaviour. Scientists studying a group of macaques began to throw them food, and the monkeys soon learned to wash the sand off it in a freshwater pool. Soon they found that sweet potatoes tasted better if they washed them in the sea instead. The scientists noticed that both these new pieces of behaviour were started by one young female, and then copied by the others, until the whole colony knew what to do.

The spot-nosed monkey is a typical example of a guenon. It lives in the rain-forests of Central Africa, in Sierra Leone and north-west Zaire, spending most of its time in the

The spot-nosed monkey is fond of the same fruits as humans, and so is treated as a pest.

trees. Its diet consists of fruit and leaves, including young growing shoots, and occasional insects. Because of its fondness for the fruits which humans grow for food, it is often treated as a pest. At 6 kg (14 lb) males weigh about half as much again as females (average weight 4 kg (9 lb)), and they use their greater strength to defend a group of between 20–40 females and young, driving other males away.

A typical mangabey is the sooty mangabey, which lives in the rain-forests of West Africa, from Senegal to Gabon. It lives mainly on the ground, though it climbs trees to find food, usually palm nuts and other fruits and seeds. It depends on untouched primary forest for its survival: sadly, this makes it typical of many small forest monkeys, which are placed in danger every time another area of forest is cut down for timber or farmland.

11

The dog-headed monkey

Although baboons are referred to as true monkeys, they look much more like dogs, walking on all fours, with a characteristic long, dog-like snout. A baboon's long jaw is an adaptation to chewing coarse grass: it leaves room for large grinding teeth at the back. Its dog-like way of walking enables a baboon to travel long distances on the ground without tiring. When it is feeding, a baboon often stands on one hand and picks grass with the other.

There are two main species of baboon. Savannah baboons live in grasslands, often near the edge of forests, all over Africa. Their close relative, the Hamadryas baboon, lives in the mountains and deserts of North Africa and Arabia, wherever it can find enough grass or thorn bushes to eat.

Savannah baboons live in large social groups with several adult males guarding the females and young. They move about together in search of food, and the males often hunt as a team, catching hares and young antelopes to add to their usual diet of grass, seeds, and fruit. Each group defends its own area against neighbouring groups, sometimes with noisy border skirmishes.

The Hamadryas baboon lives in much the same way, but each group has only one senior adult male. Young males have to leave the

Savannah baboons at a waterhole. [HBL 56–79 cm (22½–32 in); TL 42–60 cm (16½–24 in).

Left *Grooming is an important social activity among savannah baboons.*

group when they become adult, at first to join a **'bachelor'** group of other young males, and later to take charge of a tribe of their own.

The drill and the mandrill are related to baboons. They live in the rain-forests of West Africa, where they feed mainly on a diet of fruit and seeds, supplemented by occasional insects, frogs and lizards. They are conspicuous because the adults, especially the males, have brightly-coloured naked rumps. Adult male mandrills have spectacularly striped faces, making them clearly visible to any rival in the dark forests.

This mother baboon is wearing a radio collar so that scientists can follow her movements.

The gelada is the only survivor of a very ancient line, living on the grasslands of Ethiopia, East Africa. Although it looks like a baboon, its calls and other signals are quite different. Geladas live in groups consisting of one adult male and several females (often called a 'harem'); the harems join together to form large herds, with groups of bachelor males round the edge, waiting for the chance to form a harem of their own.

Colobus and leaf monkeys

Another large group of Old World monkeys includes the colobus monkeys and the leaf monkeys. Most of them are highly adapted to living in trees, with long tails to help them to steer and balance in their acrobatic leaps from branch to branch.

When the leaf monkeys evolved to eat leaves as well as fruit, they could move out of the forests into more open woodland and even **savannah**. When humans began clearing the primary forests, these leaf-eating monkeys were able to find food in crop fields, and in the secondary forest which grew back when the farmers had moved on. Although none of them is really safe, they are better able to survive the impact of humans than their more specialized fruit-eating relatives.

Hanuman langurs. [HBL 41–78 cm (16–31½ in); TL 69–108 cm (28–43 in).]

In spite of their name, only about half of the different types of leaf monkeys eat only leaves. Those that do have a special adaptation to help their digestion. Take for example the hanuman langur, which lives in the southern Himalayas, feeding mainly on leaves. Its stomach is divided into two parts. The upper part, unlike the stomach of most other animals, contains no acid. Instead, it contains **bacteria**, which cause the leaves that it eats to **ferment**. When fermented enough, the leaf pulp moves into the lower part of the stomach to be digested in acid in the usual way.

The hanuman langur is a forest monkey, but it has suffered less than many others, because it is fortunate in its human neighbours. Both Hindus and Buddhists treat it with respect, so that it can live in villages and even town centres without being harmed.

A group of colobus monkeys. [HBL 47–66 cm (19–26½ in); TL 63–92 cm (25–37 in).]

Many temples in India and Nepal have colonies of langurs living in and around them, protected and fed by the monks. The colobus monkey is not so lucky. It lives in West, Central and East Africa, among people who admire it greatly, not for itself but for its skin. It is hunted for its beautiful black and white coat, which may be sold to tourists.

The colobus monkey is a good example of the use of a tail in movements between trees. Its tail has a long fringe of hairs, so that it acts as a rudder when the animal is in mid-air. At the same time the long hairs on the side of the animal's body act almost as a parachute. Sadly, it is these long, silky hairs which make the skin so attractive to hunters.

15

Monkeys of the New World

New World monkeys are different in one important way from all Old World monkeys: most of them have a prehensile tail, with which they can grasp branches, as though it were a fifth limb. In contrast Old World monkeys use their tails only for balance and steering as they leap through the trees. New World monkeys however have no adaptations for life on the ground, unlike so many of their Old World cousins.

Spider monkeys use their tails all the time as they move about through the trees. They often let their feet hang free, as they swing along below a branch, using their hands and tail for support. Sometimes they hang by the tail

A woolly monkey from Peru shows how a tail can come in useful as a fifth hand for a more secure grasp. [HBL 52 cm (21 in); TL 56 cm (22½ in).]

alone. Spider monkeys live in small groups in tall, damp forests, keeping usually to the upper levels of the trees. They feed during the day, on leaves and ripe fruits.

Another large New World monkey is the woolly monkey. It competes with the spider monkey, for ripe fruit in the rain-forest, but it is able to eat a wider range of leaves and shoots as well. It can live in forests from sea level to as high as 3,000 m (9,000 ft).

Monkeys which eat fruit often have a problem when a tree produces a crop in an area used by several different species of monkey. Fights may develop as they compete for the food, and smaller species may be driven away. To avoid this, many of the smaller species have become specialized. They may be able to eat fruit before it is ripe enough to attract the larger monkeys, for example. The small night monkey avoids competition in a different way: it feeds mainly at night, when the other monkeys are asleep. It is the only **nocturnal** monkey in the world. Being nocturnal has an added advantage for the night monkey: the animals which hunt small monkeys, such as eagles and large monkeys, are also asleep while it is out feeding.

Many New World monkeys are very noisy. The loudest of them all is the howler monkey, a very widespread species which moves around in troops of as many as 20 animals. Its loud hooting call, which can be heard a kilometre away, warns other howler monkeys to keep away from the tree where its troop is feeding.

Opposite *The night monkey of South America.*

16

Gentle giants

Gorillas are the largest living primates, and, with the chimpanzees, the most closely related to humans. Apart from humans, they are the most intelligent land animals. However, because they are so large, so strong and so noisy, people think that gorillas are very fierce and even dangerous. In fact, they are peaceful animals, and only dangerous when they are defending their families.

There are two main types: the lowland and the mountain gorillas. Both types live in the region of Central Africa: lowland gorillas live mainly in the forests of Zaire and Gabon, and

A large silverback climbs a tree in search of a favourite food.

Vital statistics

Height Male 170–180 cm (5 ft 6 in–5 ft 10 in); female 150 cm (4 ft 11 in).

Weight Male 140–180 kg (300–400 lb); female 90 kg (200 lb).

Gestation 250–270 days.

Weaned Two-and-a-half to three years.

Sexual maturity Male 10 years, breed at 15–20; female seven to eight years, breed at 10.

Longevity In the wild, 35 years; up to 50 in captivity.

Distribution **Mountain Gorilla** Zaire, Rwanda, Uganda, up to 3,800 m (12,500 ft); **Eastern Lowland Gorilla** East Zaire only; **Western Lowland Gorilla** Cameroon, Central African Republic, Gabon, Congo, Equatorial Guinea. All species live in open forests with dense undergrowth.

The gorilla is only dangerous if someone tries to interfere with its family.

mountain gorillas live mainly in Rwanda. Although they live in different places, their lives are much the same.

Gorillas walk on all fours, using the soles of their hind feet and the knuckles of their front feet. They live in groups of about five or ten animals, or 30 at most. The leader of the group is an adult male, usually called a 'silverback' because of his colouring. There may be two or three adult females and perhaps four or five young animals making up the group, though some groups contain more females and young.

Learning a human language

Both gorillas and chimpanzees have been taught to use a human language. Koko, a gorilla, learned to communicate with her trainers in Ameslan, the American sign language used by deaf people. She could make up new sentences using the signs she had learned. Washoe, a chimpanzee, learned 30 signs in 22 months, which was remarkable enough; but when she was given an orphaned chimpanzee to look after, she taught it too to use the language.

The group stays together for years, travelling slowly around the forest floor looking for the leaves and twigs which are their main food. They have strong teeth and jaw muscles to help them crunch up enough of this coarse diet to feed their large bodies. Because adult gorillas are so heavy, only the young ones regularly climb trees.

At night, gorillas sleep in nests made from leaves and branches pulled and bent under them to make a platform or a cushion, to keep them warm and dry, and off the cold ground.

Gorillas feed on a wide variety of leaves and twigs in the forest.

Sometimes the nests may be made a little way up a tree, especially on a steep hillside, where they might roll down the slope in their sleep.

A baby gorilla can walk about 10 months after it is born, but it is not **weaned** until it is nearly three years old. Only then will its mother start another baby, so that she can give birth only about once every four years. Nearly half the babies die before they are three years old, which means that a female gorilla can produce a baby that will grow up to be an adult only about every six years. This slow breeding rate causes problems in places where gorillas are captured or killed by people, their only enemies.

Man of the woods

The orang-utan lives in the rain-forests of Borneo and Sumatra (Southeast Asia). It is a large, shaggy, red-haired ape, and the male has a distinctive baggy pouch at its throat. The male of the species is nearly twice as big as the female although no one knows for sure why this is so. The hands and feet of orang-utans are like hooks and they have very long arms, so that they can swing easily through the trees.

Unlike gorillas, orang-utans do not live in families; they are solitary creatures. A young orang-utan, however, will stay with its mother until it is at least three years old. Then it begins to wander, staying away from her for longer periods, until by the time it is about eight or ten years old it is independent. Orang-utans need such a long **adolescence** because they have so much to learn. They must know how to find fruit, and which fruits are good to eat, as well as becoming agile enough to move about in the trees without danger.

An adult orang-utan travels alone, deep in the forest. It feeds by day, mainly on fruit,

Vital statistics

Height Male 137 cm (4 ft 4 in); female 115 cm (3 ft 9 in).

Weight Male 60–90 kg(130–200 lb); female 40–50 kg (90–110 lb).

Gestation 260–270 days.

Weaned Three years.

Sexual maturity 10 years; males do not breed until about 15 years.

Longevity In the wild 35 years; up to 50 in captivity.

Distribution The rain-forests of Borneo and Sumatra.

with some leaves, insects, bark, and eggs, and even sometimes birds and squirrels. It finds water in holes in trees, taking scoopfuls to drink in its hands. It will make a nest to sleep in at night rather like gorillas do, by bending and breaking branches to make a platform, often high in a tree.

Adult male orang-utans are very aggressive towards each other when they meet. They have staring matches or crash about shaking and breaking branches, and often the display ends in a fight. To avoid too many accidental meetings therefore, the males tell each other where they are by calling loudly through the forest. The large pouch beneath an adult male's chin acts as an echo-chamber, to make his calls sound louder.

Orang-utans have to compete with humans for their food, because both like the same

The long call

Male orang-utans make a strange noise from time to time known as the 'long call'. It begins when they break off a branch and hurl it to the ground: next, they make a series of loud roars, rising to an ear-splitting bellow, before they fall quiet again, sometimes after two minutes of calling. The call is probably a warning to other adult males nearby to keep their distance.

A young orang-utan. Orang-utans move slowly through the forest, swinging from tree to tree, using their body weight to bend branches closer together.

kinds of fruit. Some of the people of Borneo are very fond of orang-utans, treating them almost like people: it is these tribes that have named them 'man of the woods'. Other tribes have hunted them for many years. Once people used to keep orang-utans as pets, but now that is illegal, and the hunting of this species has also been banned. Today the main danger to the orang-utan is **logging** which is destroying its natural habitat.

Clever little cousins

Chimpanzees, with gorillas, are our closest relations. Their senses are like our own, though they have a slightly better sense of smell. They live in communities which are divided into smaller groups, like ours. They have a thinner skull than gorillas, with a relatively larger brain, and they are very intelligent. Chimpanzees have been taught to use sign language to communicate with humans, though in the wild they manage with only 13 calls, ranging from a soft grunt to a scream.

Chimpanzee society is quite complex. Every chimpanzee is part of a large community, or clan, which may have anything from 15 to 120 members. Males usually stay with the clan where they were born, but females often join another clan when they are

Vital statistics

Height Male 100–115 cm (3 ft 3 in–3 ft 9 in); female 90–105 cm (3 ft–3 ft 6 in).

Weight Male 40 kg (88 lb); female 30 kg (65 lb).

Gestation 230–240 days.

Weaned Two to three years.

Sexual maturity Male three to four years; female 11–13 years, first giving birth at about 13–15 years.

Longevity 40–45 years.

Distribution West and Central Africa: north of Zaire River, and from Senegal to Tanzania, in rain-forests and on the savannah.

Chimpanzees eat mainly fruit, but they are fond of fresh green leaves as well.

Chimpanzees breed in many zoos around the world. These are in Singapore Zoo.

nearly ready to have their first baby. Within the clan there are smaller groups, with perhaps six members, who tend to move about together. Mothers often travel alone with their small babies, but males are more social, usually travelling with other males.

Chimpanzees feed mainly on fruit, with some fresh young leaves and occasionally flowers. Seeds are an important food during the dry season. They are fond of insects, mainly ants and **termites**. From time to time, groups of males catch and eat monkeys, pigs, and even antelope, if they can take them by surprise. They usually feed alone. If a number of them meet in a tree that has a good crop of fruit, they often squabble amongst themselves. Even after a successful hunt, the males are reluctant to share their prey.

Females have their first baby at about 15 years old. The baby is helpless for a few days, until it is strong enough to cling onto its mother's fur. After six months, the baby can ride on her back; but it cannot walk properly until it is four. It stays close to its mother until it is at least five years old, often longer. Its mother looks after it, plays with it, and often shares food with it.

Chimpanzees build nests in trees in the evening, like the other great apes. A mother shares her nest with her baby until the next baby is born, usually when the first is about five years old. Other adults sleep alone.

Another chimpanzee species, called the pygmy chimpanzee or bonobo, lives only in Zaire, south of the River Zaire. Apart from its slightly smaller build, it is very similar to its cousins elsewhere in Africa.

Using tools

Chimpanzees are famous for their skill at using tools. In the wild, this may only mean using a blade of grass to fish termites out of holes, or throwing sticks and stones at their enemies. In captivity, chimpanzees have shown much more complicated skills, such as piling up boxes to get food which has been hung up out of reach.

24

Primates in danger

Most primates in the world are in danger for two main reasons. The biggest threat comes from the destruction of their habitat, as forests are cleared to make farmland or logged for timber. Hunting, both for food and to supply the trade in souvenirs and pets, is another serious danger.

Among the rarest primates is the golden-rumped lion tamarin, from the forests of south-eastern Brazil. There are less than 100 left alive in the wild, in one reserve; but a colony of 20 captive animals is breeding well in a zoo in Rio de Janeiro, Brazil's capital city. There is a total of 100 woolly spider monkeys left, in two separate reserves in South Amer-

The destruction of the forests where they live is the greatest threat to the world's primate.

A green monkey waiting to be sold in a market in Sierra Leone. It is unlikely to live long in captivity.

ica, but they are in more danger than the tamarins, since they have never bred in captivity. Woolly monkeys are often captured to be sold as pets, which places another strain on the slow-breeding wild population.

The orang-utan population of the whole of Indonesia totals about 50,000, but only a few thousand live in protected areas (see box on page 29). The rest live in the rapidly disappearing forests outside, where they are in great danger. Apart from losing their habitat, they are endangered by **poachers**, who shoot the mothers and sell their babies as pets to merchants in Taiwan. As many as 5,000 orang-utans may be lost each year to this cruel trade.

Gorillas, too, are in double danger. Loss of habitat threatens the mountain gorilla especially, with barely 250 survivors. Another threat comes from hunters who sell pickled gorillas hands and feet to tourists, to take home as souvenirs.

Chimpanzees are trapped illegally to be sold for use in medical research. The institutions which buy them are as guilty as the hunters who trap them.

The greatest threat facing the lemurs of Madagascar is the loss of their habitat. Some species are still hunted for food, but they are all threatened by the continued destruction of the forests where they live. There are people who say that because of the loss of Madagascar's soil through **erosion**, all the primates which live there are in danger, including the humans.

Compared with the losses caused by the destruction of forests and commercial hunting, the number of primates which are killed by farmers protecting their crops is quite small: but primates as a whole are becoming so rare that not one can be spared.

Chimpanzees trapped illegally in the wild are sold to be used in medical research.

A shameful trade

In several countries of the Far East, wild primates are sold in shops, either as pets or even for food. They are usually young ones, captured after their parents have been killed, and they do not usually live very long. An orang-utan sells for £300, a gibbon £50, and some of the smaller monkeys for as little as £15. Many of the buyers are Europeans who try to smuggle the animals home with them to sell them at a profit.

Saving our relations

We have seen that the greatest threat to primates as a group is the loss of their forest habitat. The obvious defence against this is to set up reserves and national parks where the animals will be safe: but this is not so simple.

Take the gorilla as an example. In the countries where it lives, the governments need funds for much more urgent projects than saving gorillas. Where reserves have been established, they are funded by international bodies such as WWF; but often local people feel that the animals are being given land which should be for growing food.

The problem of hunting is similar. In many countries, people hunt small primates for food. If they are told that they can no longer hunt in the forest, because it is now protected by law, they may turn to poaching.

Where poachers hunt primates in order to sell their hands or skulls as souvenirs, the problem should be easier to solve—by telling tourists not to buy them, and by making it difficult for them to smuggle these items out of the country. All the same, the trade goes on, because some tourists seem unable to understand what damage they are doing.

Some primates have become so rare that their chances of survival in the wild are practically nil. Captive breeding has been successful in some of these cases. Squirrel monkeys and marmosets, for example, settle down well in captivity. Larger apes are more difficult to breed, though there are captive breeding populations of some of them, such as woolly monkeys and brown howler monkeys. It is hoped that the captive-bred animals might one day be released back into their natural habitat, when it has been made safe for them.

To make the habitat safe, ways must be found of preventing the continual expansion of humans into the forests where the monkeys and apes need to live. Two ways of achieving this are by controlling the growth of the human population, and by finding more efficient methods of agriculture, so that people need less farmland.

The only real hope for the survival of the primates, however, is education, to teach humans to respect and protect their closest relations.

Orphans of the forest

The main source of danger to all primates is the loss of their habitat. Large apes such as gorillas and orang-utans need large areas in order to survive. When the forests are cut down, they may have nowhere to find food, or they may not be able to defend territories big enough to live in.

In the forests of Borneo and Sumatra, many orang-utans are being made homeless as the area of remaining forest dwindles. These animals are being helped by money from the Indonesian Government, Frankfurt Zoo, and the Worldwide Fund for Nature (WWF) which has been used to set up rehabilitation centres. There are two such centres in Gunung Leuser National Park, in Sumatra. The park protects 6,000 sq km (2,315 sq miles) of rain-forest, with a population of about 2,000 wild orang-utans. Each centre caters for up to 20 newcomers at a time. These may be babies whose parents have been killed during tree-felling, but often they are animals which have been kept captive as pets, even though this has been illegal for over 50 years. Captive animals brought to a centre are kept in quarantine for about six weeks, to make sure that they have not caught any human diseases.

When their quarantine is over, and they have been **vaccinated**, the orang-utans are taught how to live in the jungle. Some of the orang-utans are too ill to have a chance of becoming truly wild again: they will stay in the centre for the rest of their lives. Others make a full recovery and disappear off into the jungle, free at last.

Glossary

Adolescence The process of growing up to be an adult.

Adult Fully grown.

Bachelor A male without a mate.

Bacteria Microscopic forms of life which can cause fermentation or sometimes disease.

Binocular Able to look at something with both eyes at once.

Erosion The wearing away of the land, in this case due to the removal of natural tree cover which anchors the soil.

Evolution The slow process by which species change over a very long period of time.

Evolve Undergo evolution.

Extinct No longer existing, wiped out.

Ferment To be broken down by the action of bacteria.

Great apes The gorillas, orang-utans and chimpanzees are known as the great apes, whereas the gibbons are known only as apes.

Habitat The type of place where an animal needs to live.

Logging Cutting down trees for timber.

New World North and South America.

Nocturnal An animal that is active during the night, and which sleeps during the day.

Old World Europe, Africa and Asia.

Poacher Someone who kills animals illegally for his own profit.

Prehensile Capable of grasping.

Prosimians The smallest and least-developed members of the order of primates.

Range The area of land in which an animal lives.

Savannah The tropical grasslands of Africa.

Social Acting in groups, working together.

Species A group of animals having identical characteristics.

Termite A small social insect which eats vegetable matter, a 'white ant'.

Vaccinated To be given a small dose of a disease to protect against further attacks.

Weaned Able to eat solid food.

About the author

Malcolm Penny has a B.Sc. Hons degree in zoology from Bristol University in England. He trained as a schoolteacher, but soon became involved in conservation. After working in the Indian Ocean for the International Council for Bird Preservation and the Royal Society, he moved to the Wildfowl and Wetlands Trust. Since 1973 he has been a producer of natural history programmes for Survival Anglia, the internationally-renowned wildlife film-makers based in Norwich, England. He has travelled widely, and is convinced that the future of the primates – including humans – depends on conserving their habitat.

Index

The entries in **bold** are illustrations.

Picture Acknowledgements

The publishers would like to thank the
Survival Anglia picture library
and the following photographers for the use
of photographs on the pages listed:

Richard Bailey 24; Joe B. Blossom 9, 19, 28;
Liz & Tony Bomford 8, 12 (right); Caroline
Brett 26; Bob Campbell 13, 15; J. B. Davidson 12 (left); Nick Gordon 11, 23, 27;
M. Kavanagh 5, 14, 25; Dr F. Körster 6; Lee
Lyon 18, 20; Dieter Plage 29; Dieter & Mary
Plage 7, 22; Alan Root 4, 16, 17.